ABRAHAM LINCOLN

How Kindness Made a Difference

DEBORAH KLIM

COPYRIGHT NOTICE

Abraham Lincoln: How Kindness Made a Difference

Cover and Interior Design: Derinda Babcock

Cover and Interior Illustrations: Sonnaz

Editor(s): Derinda Babcock

PUBLISHED BY: Deborah Klim, Lincolnusa16@gmail.com, 2025

Library Cataloging Data

Names: Klim, Deborah (Deborah Klim)

Abraham Lincoln: How Kindness Made a Difference / Deborah Klim

80 p. 23cm × 15cm (9 in × 6 in.)

Identifiers: ISBN-13: 979-8-9929206-0-4 (paperback) | 979-8-9929206-1-1 (trade paperback) | 979-8-9929206-2-8 (e-book)

Key Words: Children's American Civil War Era History Books; Abraham Lincoln kids book; Abraham Lincoln books for kids; children's kindness book; Teen & Young Adult President & First Family; Abraham Lincoln biography book; values books for kids

Library of Congress Control Number: 2025905997 Nonfiction

DEDICATION:

With heartfelt gratitude for the enthusiasm and support of Eliza Lea Lin and Paul Pao-Yen Lin.

APPRECIATION:

My gratitude to the following young people who donated their time to read, review, and critique this book. Their feedback was immeasurable. Thank you, Alex, Annabelle, Eden, Ellie, Genesis, and Hunter.

FOREWORD

Since quotes are from the 1800s, I have modernized the grammar and spelling for easier comprehension.

If a story has been repeated over the years, but I cannot substantiate it through more than one person, I will begin the sentence with, "According to one source." This does not mean the stories are false, as they are consistent with Lincoln's reputation and many are well known. I simply do not have more than one source to confirm the tale.

When Abraham Lincoln ran for president in 1860, he was not well-known in the United States. As a result, he was asked to write autobiographies to introduce himself to the American people, one in 1859 and another in 1860. The 1860 version is long, detailed, and written in the third person; Lincoln refers to himself as 'he.' Many quotes from these works are included and often preceded by "Years later."

Although most people picture Abraham Lincoln with a beard, he actually didn't have one for most of his life. He began to grow a beard after receiving a letter from Grace Bedell, an eleven-year-old girl from Westfield, New York. Grace had seen a picture of Lincoln and thought his face looked very thin. She suggested he grow whiskers to improve his appearance, believing it would help him win more votes.

By the time he was inaugurated in March 1861, he was the first U.S. president with a full beard.

Kindness accumulates
Kindness resonates
Kindness ripples
And sometimes triples
Its impact

CHAPTER ONE

KINDNESS IS TIMELESS

Do you recall a time when someone was kind to you? You may have felt relieved, happy, or grateful.

People long ago displayed kindness as people do today.

Kindness is not limited by social class. Whether someone is wealthy or not, kindness is shown and known.

Kindness comes in different sizes. Small acts are warm and prompt a smile. Larger acts can be life changing.

Kindness comes at different costs. A reassuring word or hug, a shout out or compliment, a fist bump, or a high five are inexpensive yet meaningful.

Then there are more expensive acts of kindness. They may involve doing a favor, lending or purchasing something for someone, or providing services for free.

Kindness can be unexpected yet so appreciated.

Abraham Lincoln valued kind acts because acts of kindness, big and small, helped him in significant ways. What a difference they made! Throughout his life, he would help others as others had helped him. Lincoln extended kindness to the rich and poor, healthy and handicapped, friend and foe. Although he saved a nation and helped to free millions of enslaved people, his acts of kindness reveal a man who is unknown to many.

CHAPTER TWO

The Early Years

1809 – 1830

Childhood to Age Twenty-One

While Abraham Lincoln is best known as the sixteenth President of the United States and the man who led the country through a bloody civil war, his story did not begin there. He was born in a small, one-room log cabin in rural Kentucky on February 12, 1809. The country was very young. Only thirty-two years before his birth, the Declaration of Independence had been issued on July 4, 1776.

Thomas Lincoln, his father, supported the family as a farmer and carpenter, while Nancy Hanks Lincoln, his mother, cared for Abe, his older sister Sarah, known as Sally, and the home. When Abe was seven years old, they left Kentucky for Indiana. Like many pioneers, his father moved west for a better life.

Years later, Lincoln wrote about this move, "Abraham, though young, was large (for) his age, and had an axe put into his hands at once." He helped to clear the land, cut trees and branches, and did whatever was necessary to create the new homestead.

He explained, "I was raised to farm work."

At nine years old, tragedy struck. His loving mother, Nancy, passed away in October 1818, after drinking milk from a cow that had eaten the poisonous white snakeroot plant. Sally, eleven years old, tried her best to replace her mother but found the responsibilities overwhelming. Needing help in the home, Thomas Lincoln left Indiana the following year to find a new wife in Kentucky.

He returned months later in December 1819, with Sarah Bush Johnston, a widow whom he had known when they were young. She brought a son and two daughters, plus much-needed furniture, books, and household goods, vastly improving the simple cabin.

Upon arrival, she discovered two neglected, dirty kids in torn clothing. Dennis Hanks, a twenty-year-old cousin of Lincoln's mother, who lived with the family, reported, "She soaped, rubbed, and washed the children clean. She sewed and mended their clothes, and the children once more looked as human as their own good mother left them." Sarah Bush Lincoln brought love and stability to the home.

Equally valuable, she offered the affection, support, and much-needed encouragement that young Abe missed. She recognized learning was important to him because she understood him. "His mind and mine ... seemed to run together, move in the same direction," she explained. To him, she was Mama. Later in life, he revealed to a family member that she "had been his best friend in this world and that no son could love a mother more than he loved her."

He read the books his stepmother brought and other books borrowed from neighbors who lived miles away. Among the books he read were *The Bible*, *Aesop's Fables*, *Robinson Crusoe*, *Pilgrim's Progress*, and *The Arabian Nights*, biographies of George Washington and Benjamin Franklin, plus grammar, math, and public speaking books. His total formal education equaled less than one year of classroom schooling. Determined to grow beyond his humble beginnings, he primarily taught himself whatever he needed or wanted to know. With that in mind, he declined the few books he thought would not add to his knowledge or enjoyment. According to his stepsister, Matilda Johnston, "Abe was not energetic except in one thing. He was active and persistent in learning … read everything he could."

While surviving on the frontier required physical strength, Lincoln was not a big fan of work that demanded hard manual labor. He wanted to expand his mind, not his muscles. He yearned, desired, to learn. Per John Hanks, his mother's cousin: "When Abe and I returned to the house from work, he would go to the cupboard—snatch a piece of corn bread— take down a book— sit down on a chair—cock his legs up as high as his head and read."

At least two of the schools that Lincoln attended in Kentucky and Indiana were called "blab schools." Typical for isolated, rural areas, the schools had no books or writing materials. As a result, the teacher called out the lesson, after which the students loudly repeated the material dozens, if not hundreds, of times, as a group and individually. Since Lincoln read out loud his entire life, the habit likely began in a blab school.

He wrote an essay for school regarding an incident that deeply upset him. When young Abe encountered a group of boys torturing a turtle by placing hot coals on its underside, he could not tolerate their cruelty. Seething with anger, he reprimanded them and rescued the poor creature. Many years later, he included the incident in a political speech. He compared tortured turtles squirming out of their shells to dishonest politicians wiggling out of their skins.

Reflecting on his limited education, in his 1859 autobiography, he wrote, "There was absolutely nothing to excite ambition for education. Of course, when I came of age I did not know much. Still somehow, I could read, write, and cipher to the Rule of Three, but that was all. I have not been to school since. The little advance I now have upon this store of education, I have picked up from time to time under the pressure of necessity."

Many people in Indiana did not know how to read. Lincoln read newspapers and mail to them. Plus, he wrote letters on their behalf. According to one source, his father asked him to read to the family, *The Life of Dr. Benjamin Franklin, Written by Himself.* For those he helped, his love of reading was a real asset.

Lincoln had a great sense of humor. He also had the unique ability to mimic accents and movements. Even as a boy, it would not be unusual for him to memorize the sermon from church. Afterward, he would go home and gather children around him as he hopped onto a tree stump and imitated the preacher in both voice and motions.

Much like his father, he loved entertaining people with stories and jokes. According to his mother's cousin, Dennis Hanks, "Sometimes, when he went to a log house-raising or corn-shucking, he would say to himself and sometimes to others, 'I don't want these fellows to work anymore' and instantly he would commence his pranks, tricks, jokes, stories—and sure enough all would stop—gather around Abe and listen, sometimes crying—and sometimes bursting their sides with laughter. He sometimes would mount a stump—chair or box and make speeches—speech with stories—anecdotes & such like thing. He never failed here."

On another occasion, Lincoln witnessed a fight begin and, according to one source, said to a friend, "Let's go over there. I'll tell a joke. That will break it up."

Throughout his entire life, he had a strong reputation for relating jokes, stories, or anecdotes to lighten the mood or to make a point.

Although Lincoln later became a lawyer, his legal education began in a very personal way. At age eighteen, he was accused of breaking the law by carrying people and their belongings in a flat-bottomed boat from the Indiana side of the Ohio River to steamships anchored in the middle.

Because the river did not have bridges, ferries (large boats or ships) carried people all the way across to the other side. Young Lincoln did not realize that ferryman John T. Dill held the license for that part of the river, which gave him exclusive rights to transport people. Angry with the teenager, Dill filed charges against him.

Constable David Turnham of Indiana issued the charge. Justice of the Peace Samuel Pate of Kentucky heard the case. As the Justice of the Peace, Pate oversaw minor legal cases and disputes.

Lincoln explained he did not realize he was breaking the law. He argued that he was not going across the Ohio River to Kentucky, only to the middle to meet steamboats that did not dock.

Since Dill's ferry never went out to those steamboats, Pate decided in favor of Lincoln. He ruled that Lincoln did not require a license because he was not crossing the river, only going to the middle.

Since by law any money earned by Lincoln before the age of twenty-one went to his father, this decision was good news for his family.

His entanglement with the law unexpectedly opened doors for the teenage Lincoln. Eager to learn, he found a willing teacher in the Justice of the Peace. Pate explained that people would be better citizens if they understood the laws that applied to them. Lincoln asked many questions while sitting with Pate on his front porch. Pate not only answered his questions and explained key legal points, but he invited Lincoln to attend his court in Kentucky. Lincoln frequently paddled his boat across the Ohio River to observe Pate's court.

Constable David Turnham, the law enforcement officer, welcomed Lincoln into his home to read "The Revised Laws of Indiana." According to Turnham, "He would come to my house and sit and read it. It was the first law book he ever saw." The Declaration of Independence and the United States Constitution, which were included in the book, especially interested Lincoln. This was likely his first exposure to these important American documents but certainly not his last.

Lincoln's interest in law extended to cases heard in the Indiana courthouses of Boonville, Rockport, and Princeton. Regardless of the distance, he willingly walked to attend court sessions in buildings that were also used for community events, concerts, and theater.

A murder trial at the Boonville courthouse left a lasting impression on the young Abraham Lincoln. Breckinridge, the lawyer representing a man accused of murder, gave a powerful final speech to the jury. Years later, when Breckinridge visited the White House, President Lincoln revealed, "I felt that if I could ever make as good a speech as that, my soul would be satisfied, for it was the best I had ever heard." Even though Lincoln was a teenager at the time of the trial, he was already dreaming of a future very different from his past.

By age twenty-one, Lincoln stood six feet four inches tall. Strong and athletic, he could out-lift, out-throw, out-jump, and out-wrestle nearly everyone in the area. Wrestling was a popular sport on the frontier. He preferred the side hold and used it to his advantage. As a young man, he reportedly engaged in about three hundred matches, losing only one match at age twenty-three. This impressive record led to his induction into the National Wrestling Hall of Fame in 1992 as an "Outstanding American," one hundred twenty-seven years after his death.

Abraham Lincoln spent fourteen years in Indiana, from age seven to twenty-one. In March 1830, his father, Thomas, decided to move the family west again. Abraham, along with his parents and other family members, embarked on a journey of 225 miles to reach their destination in Illinois. The trip required crossing the icy Wabash River, which separates Indiana from Illinois. Peter Smith of Illinois discussed the trip with Lincoln. Smith included their conversation in a letter he wrote on July 17, 1860.

"About 30 years ago, I did drive my father's ox wagon and team moving my father's family through your town of Lawrenceville. I was afoot but not barefoot. In my young days, I frequently went barefooted but on that occasion I had on a substantial pair of shoes. It was a cold day in March and I never went barefooted in cold weather. I will remember that trip through your county as long as I live. I crossed the Wabash River at Vincennes. When I came to the water, I put a favorite dog I had along into the wagon and got in myself and whipped up my oxen. (I) started into the water to pick my way across as well as I could. After breaking the ice and wading about one quarter of a mile, my little dog jumped out of the wagon. The ice being thin, he broke through and was struggling for life. I could not bear to lose my dog. I jumped out of the wagon and waded waist deep in the ice and water, got hold of him and helped him out and saved him."

When they arrived at their destination near Decatur, Illinois, Lincoln was twenty-one years old and legally old enough to leave home. Yet, he chose to wait. For the last time, he wielded his axe to help his family settle down. At age twenty-two in 1831, he decided the time had come; he prepared to leave the home of his parents. His stepmother,

Sarah, filled a cloth with food which he tied to a stick. Tossing it over his shoulder, he said his goodbyes. From that day forward, he was completely responsible for supporting himself.

CHAPTER TWO SUMMARY

ACTS OF KINDNESS THAT SHAPED LINCOLN:

1. SARAH BUSH LINCOLN: His stepmother provided love, support, and encouragement. Her presence dramatically improved his childhood from age ten onward.

2. BOOKS: The willingness of friends and neighbors to lend Lincoln books enlarged his world. When he wanted to memorize sections, he copied entire pages on boards. He later cleaned the boards off with a knife to continue writing. He enjoyed reading immensely and often referred to it as studying.

3. JUSTICE OF THE PEACE: Kentucky Justice of the Peace Samuel Pate appreciated Lincoln's curious mind. Lincoln would visit Pate at his house to learn about the law. Pate also invited him to observe his court in Kentucky, which he did frequently.

4. THE CONSTABLE: David Turnham, the law officer who charged Lincoln with breaking the law by ferrying people to the steamboats, welcomed him to his home. He allowed him to read "The Revised Laws of Indiana" many times. This book was likely his first

introduction to the Declaration of Independence and the United States Constitution.

ACTS OF KINDNESS PERFORMED BY LINCOLN:

1. TURTLE: He rescued the turtle being tortured. A great lover of animals, he often helped or protected them.

2. READING AND WRITING FOR OTHERS: For those who could not read or write, Abe was willing and able to assist.

3. THE FIGHT: He broke up a fight with humor. In those days, fights could be very violent and often led to serious injuries.

4. HIS DOG: He saved his dog from the frozen Wabash River near Vincennes, Indiana. He couldn't bear to lose him.

5. ILLINOIS: Legally old enough to leave his family when they arrived in Illinois, he chose to stay and help them settle down.

CHAPTER THREE

NEW SALEM, ILLINOIS

1831-1837

AGES: TWENTY-TWO TO TWENTY-EIGHT

In July 1831, Lincoln ended up in a small but growing village in Illinois called New Salem. In his own words, he arrived as "a friendless, uneducated, penniless boy." He described himself as a "piece of floating driftwood," taken by the current of life to wherever it landed. At its peak, New Salem was home to no more than 25 families. The village eventually had four stores, a post office, a tavern, an inn, two doctors, a private school, a blacksmith, and various craftsmen who made barrels, shoes, furniture, and hats. Founded in 1829, near a mill on the Sangamon River, New Salem was a busy frontier community during Lincoln's six years there.

The people of New Salem quickly recognized Lincoln's love of learning because he carried a book everywhere, often reading while walking. They liked his personality, especially his sense of humor. They admired his desire to improve himself. They appreciated his honesty. He helped them in any way he could. They wanted to help him as well.

Being a single man with no cabin of his own, people welcomed him to share their homes. The village cooper, who made barrels and buckets, allowed him to sleep in his shop. It was not unusual for Lincoln to head to the cooper shop and read by the light of a fire that he built with wood scraps. Whenever he worked in a general store, he would often sleep there as it was handy and available. As for meals, he usually paid wherever a meal was offered.

Caleb Carman of New Salem recalled, "He was liked by every person who knew him. While he boarded with me, he made himself useful in every way that he could. If the water bucket was empty, he filled it. If wood was needed, he chopped it and was always cheerful and in good humor. He started out one morning with the axe on his shoulder, and I asked him what he was going to do. His answer was, 'I am going to try a project.' When he returned, he had two hickory poles on his shoulders, and in a very short time, two of my chairs had new bottoms."

Having never lived in a village before, his life changed and evolved during the six years he spent in New Salem. Lincoln grew beyond the dreaded farm chores that had so unhappily occupied his youth and assumed several new responsibilities: shopkeeper, store owner, surveyor, soldier, rail splitter, postmaster, and jack-of-all-trades.

He continued to focus on learning whenever he had free time. Recognizing how important writing and speaking skills were, he sought books to help him improve. Mentor Graham, the local school master, recommended that Lincoln study Kirkham's Grammar. Lincoln discovered that John Vance, who lived on a farm six miles away, owned a copy of the book. When Vance suggested Lincoln work on his farm to earn the book, he eagerly agreed.

After returning to New Salem, Lincoln began to seriously study grammar. His friend, Bill Greene, helped by quizzing him on the material. Lincoln's hard work paid off as his writing skills improved considerably.

He decided to run for the Illinois State Legislature in March 1832, one month after his twenty-third birthday. Impressed by his strong public speaking skills and his positions on local issues, his friends encouraged him.

His campaign was interrupted, however, by the movement of Chief Black Hawk on April 5, 1832, across the Mississippi River into Illinois. Governor John Reynolds asked for volunteers to help the army force Black Hawk and his followers out of Illinois. On April 12, 1832, Lincoln volunteered to serve since the store where he was working was on the verge of closing. Friends and acquaintances from the New Salem area joined Lincoln and nine thousand other Illinois volunteers. When the time came to select a captain to lead the sixty-eight men in his company, Lincoln won by an overwhelming majority!

In a brief autobiography written in December 1859, twenty-seven years later, he acknowledged, "Then came the Black Hawk War, and I was elected a captain of volunteers, a success which gave me more pleasure than any I have had since."

While his company engaged in no battles during their thirty-day enrollment, they were highly suspicious of a Native American named Potawotami, who walked into their camp. Lincoln's men immediately grabbed their muskets and prepared to shoot.

Lincoln took a moment to read the letter he brought from General Lewis Cass stating he was a friend. Lincoln announced he was not a spy but peaceful and should not be hurt.

Again, they held their muskets high and pointed them. Lincoln stepped in front of Potawotami to protect him, causing some in the group to accuse him of being a coward.

At that, he forcefully challenged anyone to "test him." Since no one dared for his strength was known, the disruption ended and Potawotami was safe.

He returned to New Salem two weeks before the election, which allowed little time for campaigning around the county. While he lost the election of August 1832, he won 277 of the 300 votes cast by the people of the New Salem area. He found himself without a job. Years later, he explained his situation: "I was now without means and out of business, but anxious to remain with my friends who had treated me with so much generosity, especially as I had nowhere else to go."

He performed odd jobs until January 1833, when Lincoln and William Berry opened the Lincoln-Berry General Store.

While he had no money to purchase items for a store, he signed a promissory note, which meant he "promised" to pay for the goods when they sold.

According to one source, Lincoln told the following story when asked how he trained to become a lawyer.

"One day a man, who was migrating to the West, drove up in front of my store with a wagon which contained his family and household plunder. He asked me if I would buy an old barrel for which he had no room in his wagon, and which contained nothing of special value. I did not want it, but to oblige him I bought it, and paid him, I think, half a dollar for it. Without further examination, I put it away in the store and forgot all about it. Sometime after, in overhauling things, I came across the barrel, and emptying it on the floor to see what it contained, I found at the bottom of the rubbish a complete set of 'Blackstone's Commentaries.' I began to read those famous works. I had plenty of time for during the long summer days, when the farmers were busy with their crops, my customers were few and far between. The more I read, the more intensely interested I became. Never in my whole life was my mind so thoroughly absorbed. I read until I devoured them."

These books were important in the legal world. Blackstone's Commentaries on the Laws of England, a four-volume set, were originally published between 1765 and 1769. In the early years of the United States, they were heavily used. Since there were few law libraries on the frontier, the books could be carried and referenced, providing a strong understanding of the law.

Afterward, Lincoln told the story of how the books seemed to jump into his hands from the bottom of the barrel, saying, "Take me and read me. You were made for a lawyer." He taught himself law by reading books he found, bought, or borrowed.

Three years before he officially became a lawyer, Lincoln purchased a book of legal forms. His friend, Bill Greene, recalled: "...he wrote deeds, contracts and general business... never charging one cent for his time and trouble." With no lawyers in New Salem, people appreciated his assistance.

At age twenty-four, Lincoln was offered a job as the Deputy Surveyor of Sangamon County, Illinois. Since the Lincoln-Berry General Store had "winked out," a Lincoln expression meaning the store had failed, he needed the work. He knew nothing about surveying, so he borrowed two textbooks and studied hard for six weeks. He acquired the necessary second-hand tools plus a horse to travel around the county. In his own words, surveying "procured bread and kept soul and body together."

Surveyors measured and mapped land, which was important as more and more people moved to Illinois.

Between 1834 and 1836, Lincoln would measure the boundaries for farms, houses, new roads, plus five towns. In the town of Petersburg, however, he deliberately made a section of road crooked. Had he not, the home of Jemima Elmore would have ended up in the middle of the street! Since she was a hardworking widow operating a farm and raising children, he didn't think it was right to destroy her home.

Briars nipped and tugged at his legs when he surveyed in the woods. His pants ended up torn, his legs scratched and cut. So, after one surveying job, he purchased two buckskins. Hannah Armstrong, a good friend, volunteered to sew the buckskins onto his pants so the briars wouldn't tear them.

Lincoln spent considerable time at the Armstrong home. His first wrestling match in New Salem had been against Hannah's husband, Jack, considered the best in the village. Stories differ, but some witnesses suggested that Jack cheated. When Lincoln objected, Jack's friends, local bullies known as the Clary Grove boys, advanced upon him. Without hesitation, he offered to fight them one at a time. Admiring his bravery, they backed off. From that point forward, Lincoln was a welcome guest in the Armstrong home.

James Rutledge, one of the founders of New Salem, owned a general store. One day, he noticed a fellow in town walking barefooted. Rutledge offered Wadkins shoes as payment for cutting up an old house. Wadkins agreed and began the job. Lincoln heard of the arrangement and saw him working. He grabbed his own axe and joined him. When the job was done, he turned to Wadkins and encouraged him to "go get your shoes."

While living in New Salem, Lincoln became very close to Justice of the Peace Bowling Green. As the Justice of the Peace, Green would oversee minor legal cases and disputes like property damage, public disturbances, and minor assaults.

Lincoln spent considerable time at Green's farm outside of town since he often boarded there. He and Green enjoyed lengthy conversations about the law and politics, plus they loved to exchange funny stories. To encourage his interest in the law, Green lent Lincoln law books to study.

Green even advised him to run for public office despite the fact they belonged to different political parties. Like a coach, he attempted to bring out the best in Lincoln. He allowed Lincoln to try small cases in his court before he had a law license. Lincoln didn't charge for these early cases in Green's court, as he was still learning and not yet a licensed attorney. Green played such an important role in Lincoln's life that he considered Green a second father.

Similar to Indiana, some residents of New Salem were illiterate, unable to read. As he had done before, Lincoln would read newspapers and their mail to them. When he was the postmaster from May 1833 to May 1836, he walked miles to deliver an important letter if he knew someone was waiting for it. He also wrote letters for people when requested. Mentor Graham, the local teacher, reported that Lincoln once told him that, "he learned to see other people's thoughts and feelings by writing their friendly confidential letters."

In 1834, while riding to Springfield from New Salem, Lincoln encountered a harried rider. A distressed Dr. Charles Chandler stopped to explain that he urgently needed to reach the land office to register eighty acres of land that adjoined his property. He was under pressure to beat Henry Ingalls, a wealthy landowner, who wanted the same parcel of land. He revealed that because he was a man of limited means, his neighbors had collected and lent him the one hundred dollars to register the land. He disclosed that since Henry Ingalls took a different road, he had no idea how close to Springfield he might be.

Lincoln recognized that Chandler's horse had been pushed to the point of exhaustion. Although he didn't know him well, he dismounted his own horse, saying, "Here's my horse. He is fresh and full of grit. There's no time to be lost. Mount him and put him through. When you reach Springfield, put him up at Herndon's Tavern, and I'll call and get him."

Chandler gratefully accepted the offer and swiftly took off. Because of the kindness of Lincoln, Chandler arrived more than an hour before his rival, allowing him to register the land in his name. Lincoln, meanwhile, plodded along until nighttime when he finally reached Springfield. A very excited Chandler met him. He and Lincoln remained friends for the next twenty-five years.

After the Lincoln-Berry General Store failed, Lincoln owed money to the people who had supplied goods to the store. He and his partner had originally intended to pay them back when they sold the goods. With the store closed, this would not happen. One debtor, who Lincoln owed $223.24, wanted his money sooner rather than later.

He sued Lincoln in court and won on February 21, 1835. Everything he owned—his horse, saddle, and surveying equipment—was seized and auctioned off. Devastated, he skipped the auction. Without his horse and equipment, he could no longer work as a surveyor. Repaying the people he owed money would now be nearly impossible. While he also worked as the postmaster for New Salem, his pay was only fifty-five dollars a year.

Unexpectedly, a generous friend saved the day. He bought everything back so Lincoln could continue to work. You can only imagine the gratitude he felt for this monumental act of kindness and generosity. Now he could continue surveying which enabled him to repay his friend.

In his 1860 autobiography, he revealed that while living in New Salem, "He studied what he should do—thought of learning the blacksmith trade—thought of trying to study law—rather thought he could not succeed at that without a better education." While he debated which career to pursue, his interest in politics remained strong.

In 1834, at age twenty-five, Lincoln succeeded in his second attempt to be elected to the Illinois State Legislature. Since he was still paying off the debt from the store, money was tight. His wardrobe reflected his humble circumstances: simple, well-worn clothes suitable for manual labor and surveying in dense forests. Recognizing the importance of making a good impression, he asked his friend, Coleman Smoot, for help. Smoot generously loaned him two hundred dollars for a brand-new suit and traveling expenses to the state capital of Vandalia, one hundred miles away. Being elected was a big step forward. He wanted to look his best when he arrived.

During the campaign, Springfield attorney and fellow legislator, John Todd Stuart, convinced him to focus on the study of law. According to Lincoln, he "borrowed books of Stuart, took them home with him, and went at it in good earnest." As he had done in the past with other subjects he wanted to master, Lincoln began a serious study of law on his own. Once approved to practice law by the Illinois Supreme Court on September 9, 1836, Stuart welcomed him as a partner in his law firm.

The years in New Salem transformed Lincoln's life. His successes and failures taught him much about himself, while many of the close friendships he formed lasted a lifetime. Six years after arriving in New Salem, Lincoln knew the time had come to move on. Now a lawyer, he wanted to pursue his profession in the new state capital of Springfield.

At twenty-eight years old on April 15, 1837, he began the next chapter of his life.

CHAPTER THREE SUMMARY

ACTS OF KINDNESS THAT SHAPED LINCOLN:

1. CABINS: When he arrived and throughout his time in New Salem, he did not have a cabin of his own. He relied on many people for lodging during his six years there.

2. THE BARREL MAKER: The town cooper allowed him to sleep and read in his shop.

3. AUCTION: After he was sued in court and his surveying equipment plus horse, saddle and bridle were taken from him, a friend bought it all back at an auction. This allowed Lincoln to continue working while chipping away at his debt.

4. BUCKSKINS: Hannah Armstrong sewed buckskin onto his pants to prevent cuts to his legs and pants while he was surveying in the woods.

5. BOWLING GREEN: Justice of the Peace Bowling Green became a second father to him. He encouraged his interest in law and politics plus allowed him to try cases in his court.

6. SUIT: Coleman Smoot lent him $200 for a new suit and transportation to the capital, Vandalia, when he was elected to the Illinois State Legislature.

ACTS OF KINDNESS PERFORMED BY LINCOLN:

1. BLACK HAWK WAR: Protected Potawotami, Native American, when he entered the camp and was threatened by the men of Lincoln's militia company.

2. WADKINS: Assisted Wadkins in dismantling a house, so Wadkins could earn shoes.

3. BARREL OF JUNK: Lincoln took pity on the traveler who wanted to sell the barrel, as he had no room for it in his wagon. Lincoln didn't need the barrel nor did he want it. Yet, he purchased the barrel for fifty cents to help the traveler.

4. LEGAL FORMS: Lincoln purchased legal forms before becoming a lawyer. He filled them out for people at no charge.

5. SURVEYING: While surveying a road, he made a portion of it crooked so the home of Jemima Elmore and her children would not be destroyed.

6. MAIL: When postmaster, he would walk miles to deliver an important letter.

7. DR. CHARLES CHANDLER: Lincoln swapped his horse with Chandler's exhausted horse, so Chandler could purchase a piece of land next to his property. Chandler needed to make it to Springfield before his competitor.

8. LEGAL CASES: At the urging of Justice of the Peace Bowling Green, he tried legal cases in his court.

Lincoln, not a lawyer yet, did not charge his clients for his services.

CHAPTER FOUR

Riding a borrowed horse, Lincoln arrived in Springfield, Illinois, with four dollars in his pocket and two saddlebags holding all his possessions. With no place to stay or household goods, he stopped at the general store co-owned by Joshua Speed to ask how much a single bed would cost.

When told the bedding sold for seventeen dollars, he dropped his head, "It is probably cheap enough, but I want to say that, cheap as it is, I have not the money to pay. But if you will credit me until Christmas and my experiment here as a lawyer is a success, I will pay you then. If I fail in that, I will probably never pay you at all."

Joshua Speed thought, "The tone of his voice was so melancholy (sad) that I felt for him. I looked up at him, and I thought then, as I think now, that I never saw so gloomy and melancholy a face in my life."

Without hesitation, he offered to share his room above the store with Lincoln. When Lincoln asked how to reach the room, Speed pointed to a winding staircase. Up he ran, carrying his two saddlebags. Seconds later, down he came, declaring, "Speed, I have moved."

Twenty-eight years old and a new lawyer with no clients, Lincoln had little money and few possessions except for the clothes on his back and the contents of his saddlebags.

Unbeknownst to Joshua Speed, he had extended the hand of kindness to a future President of the United States. For the rest of Lincoln's life, they enjoyed a close and meaningful friendship.

The law and politics took Lincoln all over Illinois. On his way to give a speech, while riding across the open prairie, he encountered a hog trapped in thick mud. Clearly, this would not be a happy ending for the hog, but he could not stop as he needed to continue his journey. Yet he paused and looked back over his shoulder. Later he explained that the pig's eyes seemed to say, "There now, my last hope is gone." His kind heart couldn't abandon the animal, so he trudged into the mud and released him from the grip that held him tightly in place.

Joshua Speed, his good friend, wrote a book about Lincoln in 1896. He included this story:

"Lincoln had the tenderest heart for any one in distress, whether man, beast, or bird... Six gentlemen, I being one... were riding along a country road. We were strung along the road two and two together. We were passing through a thicket of wild plum and crab-apple trees. A violent wind-storm had just occurred. Lincoln and Hardin were behind. There were two young birds by the roadside too young to fly. They had been blown from the nest by the storm. The old bird was fluttering about and wailing as a mother ever does for her babes. Lincoln stopped, hitched his horse, caught the birds, hunted the nest, and placed them in it. The rest of us rode on to a creek, and while our horses were drinking, Hardin rode up."

"Where is Lincoln?" said one.

"Oh, when I saw him last, he had two little birds in his hand hunting for their nest."

"In perhaps an hour he came. They laughed at him. He said with much emphasis, 'Gentlemen, you may laugh, but I could not have slept well tonight if I had not saved those birds. Their cries would have rung in my ears.'"

Whenever the circus came to Springfield, and many did, excitement followed. Exotic animals, clowns, trapeze artists, and more paraded through town. Thrilled children desperately wanted to see the show. Lincoln, who loved animals and entertainment, was as delighted as they were. Per Olivia Leidig, a young neighbor: "Lincoln really became a king for the children of the neighborhood. It was his delight to seek out the boys and girls in reduced circumstances who were unable to purchase tickets and, with his own children, would start out for the white tents. He would hold up the smaller children so they could get a good view of the animals and other attractions."

Bowling Green, the Justice of the Peace from New Salem, who became a second father to Lincoln, passed away in 1842. Since they were so close, the family requested that Lincoln speak at the funeral. When he arose to share his memories, he managed to utter some words but not all. With tears streaming down his face, he simply sat down to mourn the man who had done so much for him.

Lincoln fiercely defended anyone who had been treated badly. In 1846, Rebecca Thomas, a 75-year-old illiterate widow who he knew from New Salem, came to him. She had sought the help of Erastus Wright to obtain a pension, a payment of money, to which she was entitled because her deceased husband had fought in the Revolutionary War. Wright assisted veterans and their families in securing pensions. When she applied, her pension was estimated to be four hundred dollars. Wright made out the papers, received the pension, and charged Mrs. Thomas two hundred dollars for his services.

She immediately went to Lincoln and explained her case. He was not pleased with Wright. Lincoln visited Wright and demanded a refund. Wright refused. Lincoln and his law partner, William Herndon, sued Wright before a justice of the peace but lost.

Still determined to help her, Lincoln took him to court. On November 16, 1846, in front of the jury who would decide the case, he dramatically related the story of the winter encampment at Valley Forge, Pennsylvania, during the Revolutionary War. Soldiers left bloody tracks in the snow from the open wounds on their cold, bare feet. Freezing without proper clothing or bedding, over one thousand men died from starvation and disease that winter.

Stretching beyond his height of six-feet-four inches, he exclaimed these men had suffered for later generations who they had released from the tyranny of English rule. Mrs. Thomas deserved the pension that her husband had earned when he left behind a young, beautiful wife to fight for freedom, their freedom. His eloquence moved the jury, which decided in favor of Mrs. Thomas. The court awarded her $35 plus costs.

Later, Mrs. Thomas approached Lincoln to ask what she owed him. "Nothing," he replied. Furthermore, he insisted on paying for her hotel room and for the coach ride back to her hometown.

In 1855, John Shelby, a young African American, worked on a steamship traveling down the Mississippi River to New Orleans. Once there, his curiosity led him to leave the boat and explore the city. Because he was Black and lacked "free papers" to prove he wasn't a slave, he was arrested and jailed. Authorities told him that he would be sold into slavery unless he could pay for his release. Desperate, John urgently communicated with his mother, Mary Shelby, requesting help.

Mary Shelby went to Abraham Lincoln, who had provided her with legal assistance in the past. She knew he helped people of color, which many lawyers did not. Lincoln and his law partner, William Herndon, appealed for assistance to the governor of Illinois who, unfortunately, insisted that he had no power over another state. A similar appeal to the governor of Louisiana also failed.

Determined to help, Lincoln reached out to a friend whose brother was an attorney in New Orleans. The attorney informed Lincoln that John Shelby's freedom could be purchased for $69.30. Lincoln and Herndon raised money from a few friends, with Lincoln contributing $40.30. At last, John Shelby was freed and returned home to his much relieved and grateful mother. Lincoln never charged Mary Shelby for his efforts.

Even simple acts prompt appreciation. Once the Lincolns no longer needed the beautiful walnut baby cradle in which they had rocked their sons, Eddie, Willie, and Tad, Lincoln brought it back to the store where he had purchased it. While he could have been paid for the cradle or exchanged it for something else, he did neither. Instead, he offered the cradle to the first clerk who could use it. George Davis was the fortunate new father who brought it home.

Reverend Noyes W. Miner, a Baptist minister who lived in Lincoln's neighborhood, could not afford a horse and carriage, which made visiting his sick and needy parishioners difficult. According to Reverend Miner, Lincoln offered his horse and carriage frequently without ever being asked.

Julia Sprigg, a widow with six children, lived in the same neighborhood as the Lincolns. Her daughter often babysat for the Lincoln boys, and Tad Lincoln loved to play at her house. During the winter months, Lincoln would bring or send over a stack of wood to help heat her home.

As he explained to Mrs. Sprigg, "We have more than we need." In the summer, he would arrive at their door with ice so the family could enjoy cool drinks. A good neighbor, Lincoln recognized where and when small gestures made a difference.

In the spring of 1858, Lincoln returned the kindness of Hannah Armstrong, who had sewn the buckskin onto his pants while he lived in New Salem. Jack and Hannah Armstrong's son, William "Duff" Armstrong, sat in a jailhouse accused of murder. Jack had recently died, so a friend of Hannah's approached Lincoln and asked if he would take the case. He accepted instantly. Lincoln had rocked Duff's cradle when he was just a babe while enjoying the hospitality of his parents. Despite the years that had passed, Lincoln felt a strong connection to the family.

Later known as the famous "Almanac Trial," Lincoln interrogated Charles Allen, the principal witness to the murder in court. Allen claimed he saw Duff commit the crime near midnight on August 29, 1857, despite standing one hundred fifty feet away. Lincoln, of course, asked how he could be certain it was Duff, considering the distance and the hour of the night. Allen responded he could see him "by the light of the moon." When Lincoln produced an 1857 Farmer's Almanac, which proved the moon was in its first quarter and sitting on the horizon that evening, the jury realized it was unlikely there was sufficient moonlight to clearly see the perpetrator. Duff was found innocent and freed.

Following the trial, a very grateful Hannah approached Lincoln to ask what she owed him for defending her son. He refused payment. She and Jack had shared their home during a time when young Lincoln didn't know where he would sleep or find his next meal. Plus, Jack and the rough and tumble Clary Grove boys volunteered to help with his earliest political campaigns going back to his first run for the Illinois State Legislature in 1832. Helping Duff was a small return for what his parents had done for him.

James O. Cunningham, a Republican politician, shared this story. Lincoln was running for the United States Senate in 1858 against Stephen A. Douglas.

"At the entrance to the Urbana fair grounds, he (Lincoln) was met by a committee of ladies and escorted to a seat at the head of the table supporting an abundance of barbecued food. As the honored guest, he took the seat prepared for him and began eating his dinner. Looking around, he saw an old woman... looking intently at him. He at once recognized her as a waiter and dishwasher at the hotel in Urbana, whom everybody knew as Granny."

"Lincoln said to her, 'Why, Granny, have you no place? You must have some dinner. Here, take my place.'"

"The old lady answered, 'No, Mr. Lincoln, I just wanted to see you. I don't want any dinner.'"

"In spite of her protestations, Lincoln arose from his seat at the head of the table and compelled her to take his place and have her dinner, while he took his turkey leg and biscuit and, seating himself at the foot of a nearby tree, ate his dinner, apparently with the greatest satisfaction. Meanwhile, Granny Hutchinson filled the place at the head of the table and ate her dinner as he had insisted she should do."

In June 1860, while Lincoln was running for president, a stranger by the name of F.A. Wood wrote to him requesting an autograph, although he clearly stated that he was not a Lincoln supporter. Mr. Lincoln replied, "You say you are not a Lincoln man, but still would like to have Mr. Lincoln's autograph. Well, here it is." Lincoln was not often personally offended even when the offense was personal. He had a way of rising above insults.

Not only kind but fair, Lincoln had performed legal work for George P. Flood pertaining to property he wanted to lease. When Mr. Flood sent him twenty-five dollars, Lincoln felt he was overpaid. Thus, the following letter: "...You must think I am a high-priced man. You are too liberal with your money. Fifteen dollars is enough for the job. I send you a receipt for fifteen dollars and return to you a ten-dollar bill."

CHAPTER FOUR SUMMARY

ACTS OF KINDNESS THAT SHAPED LINCOLN:

1. Joshua Speed: Provided a place to stay when he first arrived in Springfield. He remained four years with Speed, who became one of his closest friends.

ACTS OF KINDNESS PERFORMED BY LINCOLN

1. HOG: Lincoln saved the life of a hog when he released it from the mud.

2. BABY BIRDS: He returned the baby birds to their nest and to the care of the mother bird.

3. CIRCUS: He brought needy neighborhood children with his own boys to the circus.

4. REVEREND MINER: Lincoln lent him his horse and buggy for church work even though Reverend Miner did not ask.

5. JULIA SPRIGG: A widow with six children, Lincoln would bring over wood to heat the house in the winter and ice to cool their drinks in the summer.

6. REBECCA THOMAS: A widow from the Revolutionary War, Lincoln helped her get the pension to which she

was entitled. He never charged her. Plus, he paid for her hotel room and her coach ride home.

7. JOHN SHELBY: When jailed in New Orleans because of his color, Lincoln attempted to secure his freedom. When that didn't work, he collected the money needed to release him and paid most of the money himself. He never charged Shelby's mother for his efforts.

8. CRADLE: He donated the family cradle to the store from which he had purchased it. He instructed them to give it to the next clerk who could use it.

9. GRANNY HUTCHINSON: An elderly woman who Lincoln knew from a place where she worked came to the fairgrounds to see him. He insisted she sit in his place of honor at the head of a large banquet table and eat. He left most of his food for her and headed for a tree under which he sat and ate.

10. WILLIAM "DUFF" ARMSTRONG: Lincoln defended the son of his good friends, Hannah and Jack Armstrong, who welcomed him into their home in New Salem. The son was found innocent. Lincoln refused payment for his work.

11. F.A. WOOD: A stranger requested Lincoln's autograph during the presidential election despite making it clear he was not a supporter of Lincoln. He mailed his autograph to him anyway.

12. GEORGE P. FLOOD: Lincoln felt overpaid for legal work. He determined the value of his legal services and returned the balance to Flood.

CHAPTER FIVE

A War President

1861 - 1865

Ages: Fifty-two to Fifty-Six

Life isn't always a direct line to an illustrious end. There are many twists and turns, starts and stops along the way.

So, how did a man born in a one-room log cabin with a dirt floor in the backwoods of Kentucky end up president? The political journey to the White House began in New Salem when he ran for the Illinois State Legislature. Although he lost his first race, he won the next four terms, serving from 1834 to 1842. He later served in the United States House of Representatives in Washington, D.C., for two years.

Upon his return from the nation's capital in 1849, he abruptly shifted gears. Politics no longer dominated his world. For five years, he focused on his law practice. Lincoln admitted he had nearly lost interest in politics until the Kansas-Nebraska Act passed in 1854. This act repealed the Missouri Compromise of 1820, which had prohibited slavery in some northern states. In addition, the Kansas-Nebraska Act, championed by Senator Stephen A. Douglas of Illinois, allowed the spread of slavery into Kansas and Nebraska if the citizens of those territories voted for it.

Lincoln strongly opposed the spread of slavery. He emerged from nearly five years of political retirement focused on one thing: preventing slavery from spreading beyond the southern states. He had hoped that containing slavery in the south would eventually lead to its end. The Kansas-Nebraska Act changed everything. Angry and energized, he began speaking out.

He eventually ran against Senator Stephen A. Douglas in 1858, hoping to win his seat in the United States Senate. Lincoln and Douglas engaged in seven grueling debates, each lasting three hours. Their focus? The fate of slavery in America. The debates drew massive crowds with attendance ranging from one thousand to twenty thousand people. Lincoln revealed that he "always hated slavery" and considered it to be "a monstrous injustice." The campaign received extensive coverage in newspapers throughout the United States, as the topic of slavery interested people across the country.

Ultimately, Lincoln gained the most votes but lost the election. Prior to 1913, the state legislatures decided who won the Senate seat, not the people. They gave the victory to Douglas. Supposedly, Lincoln lamented, "Like the boy that stumped his toe, it hurt too bad to laugh, and he was too big to cry."

Two years later, in 1860, he ran against the same Senator Stephen A. Douglas and two other contenders for the presidency of the United States. He won with 39% of the popular vote and 180 electoral votes when 152 electoral votes were required to win. Not one of the southern states voted for him. Seriously divided, the country was about to rupture.

Shortly after his election, Mississippi, Florida, Alabama, Georgia, Louisiana, and Texas left the Union, the United States. Following his inauguration, Virginia, Arkansas, Tennessee and North Carolina left, seceded. They named themselves the Confederate States of America. To form their own government, they wrote a Constitution, and elected a president, vice-president, plus a Congress.

Amid all the excitement and preparations for the presidency, Lincoln received a message from a relative in Coles County, Illinois, one hundred twenty miles away. His stepmother, Sarah Bush Lincoln, wanted to see him before he left for Washington, D.C. So, on January 31, 1861, he boarded a train to say goodbye to his precious Mama.

When word got out that the president-elect was in the area, people rushed from far and wide to see him. Even school children enjoyed a day off. Everyone hoped to catch a glimpse of Lincoln, which they did at the local town hall one evening, where he mingled among them and reminisced about his childhood. Although he enjoyed seeing old friends and family, he paid special attention to his beloved Mama.

When the time came to leave, she accompanied him to the train station. The stepson, who always cherished her love and support, and the woman who adored him as a son, embraced for one last time.

Back home, he prepared for the trip to Washington, D.C. On February 11, 1861, the day before his fifty-second birthday, Lincoln began the journey. To his surprise, at the train depot, a crowd of one thousand friends, neighbors, and townspeople had gathered to see him off. He spoke from the heart:

"My friends—No one, not in my situation, can appreciate my feeling of sadness at this parting. To this place, and the kindness of these people, I owe everything. Here I have lived a quarter of a century, and have passed from a young to an old man. Here my children have been born and one is buried. I now leave, not knowing when, or whether ever, I may return, with a task before me greater than that which rested upon (George) Washington. Without the assistance of that Divine Being, who ever attended him, I cannot succeed. With that assistance I cannot fail... I bid you an affectionate farewell."

After being sworn in as president, he attempted to woo the Confederate states back by addressing their concerns in his inaugural speech. Yet President Lincoln also emphasized that he had just taken an oath to preserve, protect, and defend the Union. His attempt to calm the waters failed.

On April 12, 1861, the Confederate forces attacked Fort Sumter in Charleston Harbor, South Carolina. The battle lasted thirty-four hours and ended the next day when the Union soldiers surrendered the fort. Thus began the Civil War, a four-year nightmare. By the time the conflict ended in 1865, at least 620,000 Americans had perished from the North and the South combined, while nearly four million people were freed from slavery.

The Emancipation Proclamation, issued on January 1, 1863, became one of President Lincoln's most significant achievements during the Civil War. The proclamation declared that "all persons held as slaves" within the rebellious states "are, and henceforward, shall be free." Never before in the history of the United States had a presidential action freed slaves.

The Emancipation Proclamation had far-reaching effects. Black people and freed slaves could now enlist in the Union Army. Ultimately, nearly 200,000 Black soldiers and sailors fought. Furthermore, the Emancipation Proclamation discouraged the countries in Europe from becoming involved in the war. They had already outlawed slavery and did not want to become entangled in a war to defend it.

Referring to the Emancipation Proclamation, President Lincoln told his good friend, Joshua Speed, "I believe that in this measure, my fondest hope will be realized."

He was referring to a statement he had made in Kentucky when visiting the Speed family in 1841. Lincoln, age thirty-two years old, stated, "I have an irrepressible (unstoppable) desire to live till I can be assured that the world is a little better for my having lived in it." He realized the Emancipation Proclamation fulfilled his fondest hope that his life would have purpose, make a difference, and benefit humanity.

Despite the darkness of a civil war where family members fought on opposite sides, the bell of kindness still rang. Often related to the war, President Lincoln did what he could when he felt the cause was doable. These acts brought rare relief to a man shackled to a country whose future was no longer certain.

Out of respect for the men who fought, President Lincoln would remove his hat and nod his head when reviewing them along a parade route or in formation. For officers, he touched but did not remove his hat when saluting them. His appreciation, admiration, and gratitude for the rank and file were known to all. When he ran for reelection in 1864, eighty percent of the armed forces voted for him.

William Johnson, an African American gentleman who worked for the Lincoln family, did odd jobs and helped with the two youngest Lincoln boys in Springfield. When they left for the White House, they requested he come along; he agreed. While on the train that carried the Lincolns to Washington, D.C., he assisted the president-elect in dressing and preparing for the many public engagements at which they stopped. Lincoln was never a fan of fancy clothes and sometimes needed persuading to wear them.

Once at the White House, President Lincoln found employment for Johnson at the Treasury Department but still used his services when he needed him. After all, he was now his barber and helped to dress him for important occasions.

During the summer of 1863, the deadliest battle of the war took place in Gettysburg, Pennsylvania. To honor the fallen on the Union side, a national cemetery was established. At the dedication of the cemetery in November 1863, President Lincoln gave brief remarks known as the Gettysburg Address. Johnson accompanied him to Pennsylvania.

On the way back to Washington D.C., the exhausted president developed a headache and fever. William Johnson tended to him on the train. Upon his return, he was diagnosed with a mild form of smallpox. Johnson remained by his bedside at the White House to care for him. Two months later, thirty-year-old Johnson developed smallpox himself and was hospitalized.

When a visitor noticed President Lincoln counting money in his office, he explained about Johnson: "He is now in hospital, and could not draw his pay because he could not sign his name. I have been at considerable trouble to overcome the difficulty and get it for him, and have at length succeeded in cutting red tape... I am now dividing the money and putting by a portion labeled, in an envelope, with my own hands, according to his wish."

Sadly, William Johnson did not survive. When he passed away, President Lincoln covered the cost of his funeral and paid off the loan on his house. Mr. Johnson had been more than just a devoted employee. He had also been a respected and valued connection to the president's beloved family and to Springfield.

According to his good friend, Joshua Speed, "He never forgot anything especially any personal kindness... When he was in Kentucky in 1841... he was staying at the house of my mother... One morning when they were alone she presented him with a Bible. Years rolled forward and he was President. (My mother) sent him word that she wanted his photograph. He sent it with this sentence: 'To my very good friend, Mrs. Lucy G. Speed, who gave me an Oxford Bible twenty years ago. A. Lincoln.' It had faded from my mother's memory till she was thus reminded of it."

President Lincoln never accepted that the Confederate states were a separate country. To him, all who fought on both sides remained Americans. It was not unusual for him to visit the injured Confederate troops when he spent time at the Union hospitals. So, during three days with the Army in Maryland in October 1862, the president walked around the hospitals, including one used for injured Confederate soldiers.

Approaching them, he said "if they had no objection, he would be pleased to take them by the hand...that he bore them no malice (ill will) and could take them by the hand with sympathy and good feeling."

After a slight pause, they quietly stepped forward one by one to shake his hand. Those who could not walk, he approached their beds and assured them that everything that could be done for them would be done. He clearly cared. His deep compassion moved many.

One evening a week, President Lincoln reluctantly undertook a responsibility that especially pained him. He was given a list of military personnel who had committed crimes worthy of being court-martialed. He reviewed every case hoping to find a reason to spare lives, which he often did. His generals accused him of undermining their authority. That never stopped him. If someone fell asleep on guard duty, he thought it wasn't their fault; they had probably been walking all day and were overtired. How could their eyes not close? If they deserted, he accused their feet of going in the wrong direction. Some of these people were still teenagers. Weren't they more valuable alive?

Indiana congressman Schulyer Colfax requested a pardon for a soldier. President Lincoln responded, "Some of my generals complain I impair discipline... in the army by my pardons... but it makes me rested after a day's hard work if I can find some good excuse for saving a man's life, and I go to bed happy as I think how joyous the signing of my name will make him and his family and friends."

Whenever he was among the troops, especially after a battle, he visited the hospitals. Per Noah Brooks, a journalist who accompanied Lincoln to Virginia in 1863, he noted the president prolonged his visit to spend time at the military hospitals. "The President, with his usual kindliness of heart, insisted upon going through all the hospital tents... and shaking hands with everyone, asking a question or two of many of them, and leaving a kind word here and there. It was a touching scene, and one to be long remembered, as the large-hearted and noble president moved softly between the beds, his face shining with sympathy and his voice low with emotion. No wonder that these ... weary sufferers, far from home and friends, often shed a tear... as they returned the kind salutation (greeting) of the President..."

While president, Lincoln opened his office to politicians, job seekers, and countless citizens. Of the regular folk, he claimed, "They do not want much and they get very little. Each one considers his business of great importance and I must gratify them. I know how I would feel in their place."

He spent long hours every weekday and most Saturdays listening to their wants, desperate needs, and desires. He referred to this time as his "public opinion baths," because these visits made him aware of what was happening beyond the White House walls.

William Stoddard, a secretary to the president, remarked, "Lincoln seldom, if ever, declined to receive any man or woman who came to the White House to see him."

He helped those he could. He helped those he shouldn't, such as teenager John Bullock from Kentucky, who pleaded for the release of his brother, an injured Confederate soldier imprisoned in Ohio. President Lincoln asked, "Will he sign a loyalty oath to the Union?" The response? "No." Thinking the cause lost, the brother was shocked when, after a long silence, the president replied, "I'll do it." Stunned, he left the White House with his "heart overflowing with gratitude to the President." To Bullock, the decision displayed "how true and genuine was Mr. Lincoln's feeling of kindness towards others."

In 1864, President Lincoln's second cousin, Dennis Hanks, with whom he grew up in Indiana, came to Washington, D.C. On his way, his pocket watch was stolen, which he mentioned to Lincoln when they met. Immediately, the president opened his desk drawer and gave him a beautiful silver pocket watch. Hanks later had it engraved with his initials.

In February 1865, two women from Pennsylvania came to see President Lincoln to plead for the release of their loved ones from prison. One begged for her son; the other for her husband. They, along with many men, had been imprisoned for refusing the draft. The draft required them by law to fight in the war.

President Lincoln summoned a general into the room and asked him to obtain the names of all the men imprisoned in western Pennsylvania for refusing the draft. The general soon returned with the list. The president asked if all the men were imprisoned on the same charges. To the general's knowledge, they were.

"Well, then," said President Lincoln, "these fellows have suffered long enough, and I have thought so for some time… I believe I will turn out the whole flock. So, draw up the order, general, and I will sign it."

The women left, thrilled to learn their loved ones would soon be released from prison.

After the ladies departed, his devoted friend, Joshua Speed, who had observed the interaction, remarked that the president placed himself under tremendous stress by agreeing to see anyone and everyone. President Lincoln replied, "… to tell you the truth, that scene is the only thing today that has … given me any pleasure. I have, in that order, made two people happy and alleviated the distress of many a poor soul whom I never expect to see. Speed, die when I may, I want it said of me by those who know me best that I always plucked a thistle (weed) and planted a flower when I thought a flower would grow."

The Civil War began to wind down after General Robert E. Lee and his Confederate Army of Northern Virginia surrendered to General Ulysses S. Grant, General of the Army of the United States, on April 9, 1865. After four years of a brutal, heart-wrenching war, President Lincoln finally felt the weight dropping from his shoulders.

The relief did not last long. Six days later, on the morning of April 15, President Abraham Lincoln died from a gunshot wound inflicted the night before at Ford's Theatre by actor and Confederate sympathizer, John Wilkes Booth.

President Lincoln's legacy extends far beyond his tragic end. His rise from a one-room cabin to the presidency proved to the nation and to the world that America is a land of opportunity.

In comments to Ohio soldiers on August 22, 1864, he claimed, "I happen temporarily to occupy this big White House. I am a living witness that any one of your children may look to come here as my father's child has."

Through his leadership, the 'United' States remained united as one nation, undivided, while nearly four million enslaved people experienced freedom for the first time.

Lincoln's life journey reflected his own never-ending determination to improve himself with the support of family, friends, neighbors, and others. So many people cleared his path through acts of kindness, minor and major. By encouraging and supporting his interests, they helped him to fulfill his ambitions.

Equally as generous, Lincoln aided others whenever and however he could. While some people asked for assistance, many did not. He simply saw a need, and without fanfare, he stepped up. He did not draw attention to himself or ask anything in return. The act was its own reward.

During the most difficult White House years with a civil war raging, he assisted the helpless and hopeless while showing compassion to those on both sides of the conflict.

In the end, he touched many lives, saved a nation, and freed millions.

CHAPTER FIVE SUMMARY:

ACTS OF KINDNESS THAT SHAPED LINCOLN:

1. MRS. LUCY SPEED, Joshua Speed's mother, gave Lincoln an Oxford Bible in 1841 when he visited her home in Kentucky. After he became president, she requested a picture of him. He wrote a note upon the photograph and mentioned her kind gift to him. She had completely forgotten about the Bible.

ACTS OF KINDNESS PERFORMED BY LINCOLN:

1. SARAH BUSH LINCOLN: On January 31, 1861, president-elect Abraham Lincoln, at the request of his stepmother, stopped all preparations for the presidency to travel one hundred twenty miles to see her and say goodbye. His father had already passed away in 1851.

2. RESPECT: For the regular soldier, President Lincoln removed his hat when they passed in a parade or formation. To them, he showed the ultimate respect.

3. WILLIAM JOHNSON: An African American gentleman who worked for the Lincolns traveled from Springfield, Illinois to Washington, D.C. with them. When Johnson contracted smallpox and was

hospitalized, he asked President Lincoln to obtain his pay check and handle his bills. When he passed away, the president covered his funeral expenses and paid off the loan on his house.

4. UNION TROOPS: Whenever he could, he visited the troops, including those who were hospitalized, to express words of care, comfort, and encouragement.

5. CONFEDERATE TROOPS: While President Lincoln never officially recognized the Confederate States of America as a separate country, he showed compassion for all wounded soldiers, regardless of their allegiance.

6. COURT MARTIALS: He did everything he could to save men from being court-martialed. If a reason could be found to spare a life, he found it or made it up.

7. WHITE HOUSE VISITORS: He seldom refused to see anyone who came to the White House to see him.

8. JOHN BULLOCK: John, a Kentucky teenager, came to the White House to plead for the release of his injured brother from a Union prison. Despite the fact that his brother refused to take a loyalty pledge to the Union, President Lincoln freed him.

9. DENNIS HANKS: When his mother's cousin visited President Lincoln in the White House, he revealed that his watch had been stolen during the trip to Washington, D.C. President Lincoln immediately replaced it.

10. DRAFT DODGERS: Men in Pennsylvania, who refused to fight in the war despite being drafted, were sent to prison. When two women came to the White House

to plead for the release of their loved ones, President Lincoln released not only them but all those who remained in prison for avoiding the draft in western Pennsylvania.

TIMELINE OF ABRAHAM LINCOLN'S LIFE

FEBRUARY 12, 1809: Abraham Lincoln is born in a one-room log cabin with a dirt floor near Hodgenville, Kentucky. He is the second child of Thomas Lincoln and Nancy Hanks Lincoln. Sarah, known as Sally, was born two years earlier.

DECEMBER 1816: At age seven, the Lincoln family moves to Indiana. Indiana is a "free" (non-slave owning) state. In 1860, Lincoln notes that the family's move to Indiana was "partly on account of slavery" but mainly due to land title difficulties. This meant that many, unrelated people could own the same piece of land which created problems. The family stays in Indiana for fourteen years.

OCTOBER 5, 1818: Nancy Hanks Lincoln, mother of Sally and Abraham, dies because of milk sickness. Eleven-year-old Sally attempts to run the household that includes her father, nine-year-old brother, Abe, and nineteen-year-old cousin, Dennis Hanks.

DECEMBER 2, 1819: Lincoln's father marries Sarah Bush Johnston, a thirty-one-year old widow from Elizabethtown, Kentucky. She and young Abe grow very close. He calls her Mama. She brings with her children John (b. 1810), Matilda (b 1811) and Elizabeth (B 1807).

MARCH 14, 1830: Traveling by ox-carts, the Lincoln family moves from Indiana to Illinois. Lincoln, age twenty-two, leaves the home of his parents from here.

JULY 1831: Lincoln arrives in New Salem, "a piece of floating driftwood," as he notes in an autobiography written in 1860. Roughly twenty to twenty-five families live there at a time.

1831: Lincoln and William G. Greene work as store clerks in New Salem for Denton Offutt. Both clerks sleep in the back of the store.

MARCH 9, 1832: At age twenty-three, he announces a run for the Illinois State Legislature.

1832: He joins the militia for the Black Hawk War. He is elected captain of his company.

JULY 1832: Returns from the Black Hawk War with only two weeks left to campaign for the Illinois State Legislature.

AUGUST 6, 1832: Loses his first race for the Illinois State Legislature. Finishes eighth among thirteen candidates with four seats available. He wins 277 out of 300 votes in the precinct that includes New Salem.

1832: Becomes a partner in a New Salem general store with William F. Berry.

1833: The Lincoln-Berry General Store fails and leaves Lincoln deeply in debt. (The store, he laments, "winked out.") Considers becoming a blacksmith or a lawyer. Works as a hired hand and begins to write deeds and mortgages for neighbors for free. Boards with different families and moves every few months.

MAY 1, 1833: President Andrew Jackson appoints him postmaster of New Salem. He serves until the post office is moved to nearby Petersburg in 1836.

1834: He works as a surveyor for three years. This job according to Lincoln "procured bread, and kept body and soul together."

AUGUST 4, 1834: He wins race at age twenty-five for Illinois State Legislature, running second place out of thirteen people with four seats available. Begins study of law in earnest. Serves in the state legislature from December 1, 1834 to December 8, 1839, winning four terms.

NOVEMBER 19, 1834: Lincoln is sued and loses surveying equipment, horse, saddle, and bridle. A friend attends auction and buys them back for him.

JANUARY 1835: The death of Lincoln's former store partner, William F. Berry, increases his debt to $1,100 (equivalent to $40,000 in 2025). He now has to pay the amount Berry owed people. Referring to this as his "national debt," he finally repays everyone in 1848 when he becomes a member of the United States House of Representatives in Washington, D.C.

SEPTEMBER 9, 1836: Lincoln receives license to practice law. Age twenty-seven. He practices law from 1836 until 1860, when he is elected president.

APRIL 15, 1837: Moves to Springfield on a borrowed horse to practice law with John T. Stuart.

1837: State capital moves from Vandalia to Springfield.

1841: Joshua Speed's father has died and his mother needs help with family matters. During the summer of that year, Lincoln visits Farmington, the Speed family home. He stays with the family for a few weeks. During this visit, Mrs. Lucy Speed, Joshua's mother, gives Lincoln a Bible as a gift.

AUGUST 3, 1846: Lincoln wins a two-year term to the United States House of Representatives in Washington, D.C.

MARCH 1849: Lincoln completes his only term in the United States House of Representatives in Washington, D.C. Returns to Springfield to practice law. Later, in a presidential campaign statement, he writes, "From 1849 to 1854… I practiced law more assiduously (with more attention and determination) than ever before." Lincoln focuses on his family and law practice. Lincoln does not run for any political office during this time period.

MAY 30, 1854: President Franklin Pierce signs the Kansas-Nebraska Act into law. Stephen A. Douglas, Senator from Illinois, is instrumental in its passage. The Act repeals the Missouri Compromise of 1820 which limits the spread of slavery. Lincoln comes out of political retirement, as he disagrees wholeheartedly with the spread of slavery beyond the southern states.

AUGUST 26, 1854: Lincoln makes first speech against the Kansas-Nebraska Act.

MAY 1858: William (Duff) Armstrong, son of New Salem friends Jack and Hannah Armstrong, is found innocent of murder. Lincoln defends him and uses an almanac to discredit the testimony of a key witness. Lincoln does not charge for his legal services.

JUNE 16, 1858: The Republican Party nominates Abraham Lincoln as their candidate for the United States Senate against Democrat Stephen A. Douglas. Age forty-nine.

AUGUST 21, 1858: Lincoln and Stephen A. Douglas debate for the first time. Six debates follow. Audiences at debates range from 10,000 to 15,000 people with two exceptions. At Jonesboro on September 15 approximately 1,500 people attend while at Galesburg on October 7, the audience swells to 20,000.

NOVEMBER 2, 1858: Despite Lincoln winning the popular vote by 3,402 votes, Stephen A. Douglas defeats Lincoln. The Illinois State Legislature, not the popular vote, decides the winner. The Seventeenth Amendment to the Constitution in 1913 changes the law so the popular vote elects senators, not their state legislatures.

JANUARY 5, 1859: The Illinois State Legislature reelects Stephen A. Douglas to the Senate by a vote of 54 to 46.

MAY 18, 1860: Lincoln is nominated by the Republican Party to represent them in the upcoming presidential election.

NOVEMBER 6, 1860: Lincoln wins the presidential election with 39% of the popular vote and the majority of electoral votes: 180 out of 303. A majority of electoral votes is required to become president. The popular vote, while counted, does not decide who wins.

DECEMBER 20, 1860: South Carolina votes to leave the Union (United States). Florida, Mississippi, Alabama, Georgia, Louisiana, and Texas secede (leave) within two months.

JANUARY 31, 1861: Lincoln visits his beloved stepmother, Sarah Bush Lincoln, at her home in Coles County, Illinois, 120 miles from Springfield.

FEBRUARY 11, 1861: President-elect Abraham Lincoln leaves Springfield, Illinois for Washington, D.C.

MARCH 4, 1861: Lincoln takes Oath of Office in Washington, D.C. He is now president.

APRIL 12, 1861: Confederates open fire on Fort Sumter, Charleston, South Carolina and assume control.

APRIL 17, 1861: Virginia leaves the Union and is followed within five weeks by North Carolina, Tennessee, and Arkansas forming the eleven Confederate States of America.

JANUARY 1, 1863: President Lincoln issues the Emancipation Proclamation which frees all slaves in the rebelling states. Before signing the proclamation, he reportedly said, "I never in my life felt more certain that I was doing right than I do in signing this paper. If my name ever goes into history, it will be for this act and my whole soul is in it." His fondest hope has been that his life would have purpose and benefit humanity.

NOVEMBER 19, 1863: President Lincoln gives the famous Gettysburg Address at the dedication of the Gettysburg National Cemetery in Gettysburg, Pennsylvania. He develops varioloid (a mild form of smallpox) on the train ride home and is bedridden for three weeks. William Johnson cares for him.

APRIL 9, 1865: General Robert E. Lee surrenders to General Ulysses S. Grant at Appomattox Courthouse in Virginia.

APRIL 11, 1865: President Lincoln makes last public speech from a window of the White House.

APRIL 14, 1865: While watching the comedy, "Our American Cousin," actor and Confederate sympathizer, John Wilkes Booth shoots President Lincoln at Ford's Theatre.

APRIL 15, 1865: President Lincoln passes away from his injuries.

APRIL 19, 1865: A funeral service for President Abraham Lincoln is held in the White House, after which his remains travel by train on a 1,654-mile journey to Illinois. The final burial takes place on May 4, 1865, in Oak Ridge Cemetery in Springfield, where President Lincoln lies to this day in the Lincoln Tomb.

RESOURCES

Reynolds, David S. *Abraham Lincoln In His Times*. New York: Penguin Press, 2020

Speed, Joshua Fry. *Reminiscences of Abraham Lincoln*. BIG BYTE BOOKS, 2014

White, Ronald C. *Lincoln in Private*. New York: Random House, 2021

Wilson, Douglas L. *Honor's Voice: The Transformation of Abraham Lincoln*. New York: Alfred A Knopf, 1998

Wilson, Douglas L. and Rodney O. Davis. *Herndon's Informants: Letters, Interviews, and Statements about Abraham Lincoln*. Urbana and Chicago: University of Illinois Press, 1997

The Lehrman Institute. "Abraham Lincoln's Personality." Abraham Lincoln's Classroom.

DEBORAH'S OTHER BOOK

Nana Has Cancer, But Cancer Doesn't Have Nana

ABOUT THE AUTHOR

Deborah Klim began the study of presidential history during her teen years. She has since traveled throughout the United States, visiting presidential libraries, museums, and birthplaces.

Her interest in Abraham Lincoln developed in 2010 following a talk by Doris Kearns Goodwin at the John F. Kennedy Presidential Library in Boston. Goodwin's portrayal of Lincoln in "A Team of Rivals" revealed a multifaceted character: tough but tender, humane but principled, funny but focused. Fascinated, Deborah decided to devote her time and attention to Abraham Lincoln exclusively.

In 2023, Deborah traveled from Colorado to Springfield, Illinois, to provide tours at the Lincoln Home National Historic Site and the Lincoln Tomb State Historic Site. This hands-on experience allowed her to immerse herself in Lincoln's history and share it with others. She returned to the Lincoln Home in 2024, and hopes to visit often in the future.

Deborah's interactions with visitors from across the country and around the world at the Lincoln Home, where Abraham and Mary lived for seventeen years, inspired her to write a book. She noticed people were most interested in the personal stories that revealed the man behind the legend. They loved the small details that brought him to life and made him relatable.

Since kids often asked the best questions, she decided to target middle and high school students. Thus, *Abraham Lincoln: How Kindness Made a Difference* was born.

Contact Deborah at Lincolnusa16@gmail.com

www.ingramcontent.com/pod-product-compliance
Lightning Source LLC
Chambersburg PA
CBHW051550120626
46551CB00013B/1454